# Find the Sock

Alexandra Behr
Illustrations by Jared D. Lee

HAMPTON-BROWN

2

On Berry Hill
Rick tells Jack,
"Find the sock, just the sock."

"Good dog, Jack!
But that's a rock.
Give the rock to me.
Find the sock, just the sock."

"Good dog, Jack!
But that's a box.
Give the box to me.
Find the sock, just the sock."

"Good dog, Jack!
But that's a bell.
Give the bell to me.
Find the sock, just the sock."

"That's it, Jack!
That's the sock!
Give the sock to me."

On Berry Hill,
Rick tells Jack,
"Find the sock, just the sock."